AMERICAN
COLONIAL
HOMES

A Pictorial History

JOHN BURDICK

COURAGE
BOOKS

AN IMPRINT OF RUNNING PRESS
PHILADELPHIA · LONDON

9 8 7 6 5 4 3 2 1
Digit on the right indicates the number of this printing.

Library of Congress Catologing-in-Publication
Number 97-66815

ISBN 0-7624-0204-0

This book was designed and produced by
Todtri Productions, Ltd.
P.O. Box 572, New York, NY 10116-0572

Author: John Burdick

Publisher: Robert M. Tod
Editorial Director: Elizabeth Loonan
Book Designer: Mark Weinberg
Senior Editor: Cynthia Sternau
Project Editor: Ann Kirby
Photo Editors: Edward Douglas, Laura Wyss
Typesetting: Command-O Design

Printed and bound in Singapore

Published by Courage Books, an imprint of
Running Press Book Publishers
125 South Twenty-second Street
Philadelphia, Pennsylvania 19103-4399

CONTENTS

INTRODUCTION

As much as histories of religion and government, biographies of famous individuals, and museums filled with artifacts and first-person accounts, houses tell the story of America. One can "read" a house as if it were an account of ancestral heritage, a statement of religious and political convictions, an expression of personal aesthetics, or a description of the locality in which it is built—the climate, the natural resources, the cultural norms and expectations. The stories of the European settlers of America are codified in the shapes, roofs, exteriors, and furnishings of their houses. These stories are not always coherent and consistent; one architectural element of a single house might express longing for the old country, another the vision of new values and social orders. From the small and pragmatic timber houses of Jamestown and

RIGHT: Shown is the home of Revolutionary War hero Ethan Allen, leader of the famous Green Mountain Boys, and promoter of the independence and statehood of Vermont. *Ethan Allen Homestead, Burlington, Vermont*

LEFT: For all its size and grandeur, the interior of Mount Vernon amply reflects the personal qualities for which Washington was known— austerity, humility, and reserve. *Mount Vernon, Fairfax County, Virginia*

ABOVE: **The Hamilton House in South Berwick, Maine, overlooks the Piscataqua River, and is a veritable museum of fine furniture and classical architecture. The house was built by Jonathan Hamilton in 1787. *Hamilton House, South Berwick, Maine***

the raw elements and profound uncertainties of a new world. The history of human civilization, from basic survival to established culture, is recapitulated, in miniature, every time a new frontier is settled.

Certainly, the original European settlers of America were hardly noble savages, or free of cultural biases and preferences. They brought with them a well-established religion, artistic sensibility, and social structure—those facets of European culture they wished to escape and those they wished to preserve. But the trauma of settlement tends to return people to a primitive state, to primal concerns. To speak of the colonial "style" of architecture is to speak of a timeless anti-style, the style of people who could little afford to concern themselves with architecture as aesthetics and expression. Theirs was a style that arose from some simple and elemental questions: How do we secure safety and shelter in this climate, using these abundant materials and these tools? Each transplanted culture answered those questions in its own way, and thus there is both the splendor of diversity in American colonial homes, and the unmistakable element of commonality.

Plymouth to the grand Georgian estates that were the abode of choice among the wealthy in all colonies, the evolution of American houses parallels the evolution of America.

History tells us that America beckons the oppressed, poverty-stricken and profit- or adventure-hungry with promises of opportunity, unlimited resources, and the freedom of the uncharted frontier. In most cases, that promise is as much wishful myth as fact; every generation of immigrants discovers that America represents not so much a paradise as the challenge to build one from scratch. Perhaps the central truth of immigration is that one must first move backward to move forward, sacrifice—or at least temporarily suspend—the pleasures and foundations of an established culture and face, as if starting over,

Historically, the colonial period stretches from the first European settlements to the Revolutionary War. Architecturally, "colonial" refers to the earliest, generally medieval-styled houses of the first settlers. Around, though not precisely in, 1700, the colonial house style gave way to the Georgian, the Renaissance-influenced classical style that would dominate American architecture in the eighteenth century. If this widely-accepted terminology is somewhat confusing, so be it, for there is considerable cause for confusion in the history of American homes as well. The colo-

nial style, for example, continued to be produced well after the ascendancy of the Georgian and the American Revolution. The famous colonial revival of the late nineteenth and early twentieth centuries was, in reality, primarily a Georgian revival.

Aristocrats and indentured servants, religious extremists and opportunistic merchants, agents of the king and banished rebels—all join forces to tell the story of early America, and all expressed their visions and versions of America in where and how they chose to live.

FOLLOWING PAGE: **The Kitchen at Shirley. Shirley Plantation was, for a time, the home of Confederate General Robert E. Lee's mother.** *Shirley, Charles City, Virginia*

LEFT: **More colonial houses exist today in New England than in any other region of the United States, and the historic town of Deerfield, Massachusetts, has twelve period houses that are open for public viewing. Among these is the Sheldon-Hawks House, circa 1743, and by no means the town's oldest building.** *Sheldon-Hawks House, Deerfield, Massachusetts*

CHAPTER ONE

NEW ENGLAND

Having Undertaken, for the glorie of God, and advancemente of the christian faith and honour of our king and countrie, a voyage to plant the first colonie in the Northene parts of Virginia . . .

—FROM THE MAYFLOWER COMPACT

The *Mayflower* missed northern Virginia, its intended destination, by a good distance, landing instead at Provincetown at the tip of Cape Cod on November 21, 1620. Some call it navigational error; others insist that the northern drift was intentional, a measure meant to insure that the pilgrim settlers would be far removed from the Virginia Company settlements and their jurisdiction. The Separatists, as the pilgrims were originally known, had suffered persecution and ostracization in England and grim poverty during their sojourn in Holland. This land would be theirs and theirs alone. In any case, they arrived just in time to meet the New England winter, a harsh welcome to the New World.

As the Anglican Church solidified its political and religious power in England, King James I ordered the harassment and imprisonment of Puritan dissenters, Protestants who attempted through non-cooperation to purify the church of its Catholic strains and rituals. The most obstinate and independent of the nonconformists were known as Separatists or Brownists, after one of

BELOW: **Arguably the oldest surviving frame house in the United States, the Fairbanks House also illustrates well the peculiar tendency of colonial houses to sprout an odd variety of additions over the years. The house belonged to the prosperous Jonathan Fayerbanke, and its changes and additions mirror his ascent in the world.** *Fairbanks House, Dedham, Massachusetts*

LEFT: **The Jethro Coffin House, Nantucket's oldest, defines the features of the New England saltbox with its small, medieval windows and long, sloping rear roof. The house also features an inverted horseshoe chimney decoration which, some say, was intended to keep witches from flying down the flue.** *Jethro Coffin House, Nantucket, Massachusetts*

RIGHT: Lawyer, farmer, and eventually president, John Adams ran his legal practice out of this room. In the same house, John Quincy Adams was born in 1767. He would later become the sixth president of the United States. *John Adams' Home, Quincy, Massachusetts*

BELOW: The property upon which this house stands had been in the Adams family since 1720, when it was purchased by John Adams' father, Deacon John Adams. John and Abigail Adams moved into this house in 1764 and lived in it for over twenty years. *John Adams' Home, Quincy, Massachusetts*

their early leaders, Robert Browne. Unlike the Puritans, who opposed the Anglican Church but not the concept of a church-governed nation, the Separatists rejected the notion of the church state entirely, choosing first to establish an isolated community and church in Scrooby, Nottinghamshire, and later, after much harassment and criticism, to flee to Holland in 1608.

In Holland, they found the tolerance and freedom of worship that they desired but not the means by which they could support themselves. First in Amsterdam and later in the university town of Leyden, the exiles suffered great hardships because their alien status precluded them from gainful employment. Many chose to return to

prison in England rather than to endure their penurious liberty in Holland. They also witnessed with some alarm the dissipation of their cherished traditions into the Dutch culture that surrounded them; they were especially disturbed by the corrupting influence on their children. In addition, Holland's truce with Spain was to expire in 1621 and war was imminent, a threatening prospect to a colony of perennial outsiders.

Thus, under the guidance of William Bradford, among others, the Separatists undertook a voyage to America. With a land grant provided by the London Company and money loaned by independent "adventurers," the Pilgrims set sail on September 16, 1620 aboard the *Mayflower*. From the outset motives were mixed. The Separatists may have wanted a place to worship without interference, but their financiers were more interested in profit than in the glorification and advancement of Christianity. Still, the Pilgrims saw their mission as essentially sacred and mandated by God, a point made repeatedly by Bradford in his magnificently detailed account, *The History of Plymouth Plantation*. In this light, all hardships they would encounter, and they knew there would be many, were tests of their will and devotion.

RIGHT: The Hoxie House in Sandwich, Massachusetts, is believed to be the oldest house on Cape Cod. It is in many ways representative of the early New England colonial style, with its simple, sturdy construction and steep-pitched roof. *Hoxie House, Sandwich, Massachusetts*

THE PLYMOUTH SETTLEMENT AND BEYOND

Many passengers died aboard the *Mayflower*, a portent of the fate that awaited the Pilgrims in New England. During the first winter at Plymouth, well over half the settlers succumbed to starvation and disease. All might have perished had not some native tribes provided corn and instructed the Pilgrims in planting techniques. Not all relations with natives were friendly, however. Chief Canonicus of the Narragansett tribe sent Governor Bradford a bundle of arrows wrapped in snakeskin, a symbolic declaration of war. When Bradford replied with a bundle of bullets, the Narragansetts reconsidered.

By the spring, conditions at the settlement had stabilized and the Pilgrims got down to the business of building a community. Originally, the

BELOW: **The much-modified and expanded Paul Revere House was bought by Revere in 1770, although it was built nearly a century earlier. The house now stands wedged between more modern buildings.** *The Paul Revere House, North Square, Boston, Massachusetts*

Separatist leaders had envisioned a communal plantation with no individual property, a reflection of the belief that theirs was a community supervised by God. The communal system, however, spawned inequity and resentment, and in 1623, Bradford abolished it, allotting an acre of farming land to each family. With corn as a staple and, at the beginning, as a currency as well, the Pilgrims repaid their debt to the London merchants that had financed their colony. Population grew slowly but steadily, resulting in the growth of independent villages, each with its own church and pastor. In spite of overwhelming difficulties, the Pilgrims had taken root.

Colonial New England might have remained a sparsely populated and fervently religious settlement had not deteriorating social conditions in England inspired a flood of Puritans to follow in the Pilgrims' wake. A widening gap between rich and poor, and continued religious persecution compelled many English tradesmen and artisans, landowners and yeoman, to seek their fortunes elsewhere. These Puritans, less extreme in their religion than the Separatists and more worldly in their aspirations, founded the Massachusetts Bay Company, later renamed the Massachusetts Bay Colony. Under the leadership of John Winthrop, the colonial enterprise hastened the spread of settlements and sparked the international economy of New England.

The first great migration of the English to New England took place between 1630 and 1643. Although this is still very much viewed as the flight of persecuted Puritans, of the estimated 16,000 English people to emigrate during this period, only about 4,000 were actually Puritans. Thus, while the Church still served as the spiritual and civic center of each town, Bradford's notion of a colony of the humbly devoted was already a distant memory. New England's economy grew rapidly as a result of the fur trade, lumber mills, and fisheries. Over these thirteen years, twenty-two towns were founded, including Boston and Salem. Some say that present-day New England still resonates

LEFT: The Stockbridge Mission House was built in the early 1730s when several Boston families, under the leadership of Reverend John Sergeant, moved to the Berkshires to spread Christianity and the English way of life among the local Housatonic Indians. *The Mission House, Stockbridge, Massachusetts*

LEFT: Isaac Royall's famous mansion is reputedly based on a house in Antigua that Royall admired. Whether this is true or not, the Royall House remains one of New England's most ornate and decorated Georgian homes. *Isaac Royall House, Medford, Massachusetts*

with the character and mythology of the small band of religious Separatists that founded it. This may well be the case, but, in reality, the Separatists' world view and lifestyle ceased to define political, social, and economic life in New England a mere decade after their arrival.

Logic suggests that population growth and the hunger for new frontiers and industries sparked the spread of English settlement into territories outside of modern day Massachusetts. In several instances, however, religious conflicts and subse-

quent banishments were equally responsible for the dispersal of the English throughout New England. The most famous case is that of Roger Williams, a once fairly typical Puritan settler who would become the founder of Rhode Island and Puritanism's harshest critic. Such figures as Williams, Anne Hutchinson, and Thomas Hooker were instrumental not only in the development of Rhode Island and Connecticut but in the growth of Puritan opposition and alternative churches and governments. By the end of the seventeenth century, Rhode Island, Connecticut, New Hampshire, and Maine were all thriving colonies. New England culture, however, was characterized by internal tensions—the sacred and the secular, separatism and expansion, the stoic humility of the Pilgrim way and the enterprising and worldly spirit of those who followed.

LEFT: The Sheldon-Hawks House features a low-standing doorway with several typically Georgian features. Inside, the building is displayed a superb collection of antique furniture. *Sheldon-Hawks House, Deerfield, Massachusetts*

ABOVE: Like so many of the early colonial houses of New England, Deerfield's Allen House visibly bears the marks of years of modifications, with additions and wings growing out of an essentially modest colonial core. *Allen House, Deerfield, Massachusetts*

RIGHT: This modest colonial house built by Samuel Hait (Hoyt) in 1699 is the oldest standing structure in downtown Stamford. Like so many early colonial homes, the Hoyt-Barnum House underwent many changes over the years, reflections of the differing needs and means of its owners. *Hoyt-Barnum House, Stamford, Connecticut*

RIGHT: Built in 1692 by David Buttolph, the Buttolph-Williams House was considered a mansion at the time of its construction. In the eighteenth century, the house was occupied by Daniel Williams. *The Buttolph-Williams House, Wethersfield, Connecticut*

EARLY COLONIAL HOUSES OF NEW ENGLAND

In such conditions as are faced by settlers, building styles tend to be determined by a few simple and elemental questions: What materials are available? What architectural features do climate and other natural conditions dictate? What technologies and techniques are familiar and practical? As survival becomes less of an issue, such matters as culture, taste, and preference assume greater importance, and distinct styles of architecture, reflecting discrete styles of living, emerge.

The first homes of the New England settlers were simple and sturdy in construction, and medieval in character. In the cities of England, the medieval style had long since been replaced by the classicism of the Italian Renaissance. But the settlers of New England were generally simple townsfolk, farmers, and artisans without great wealth or formal education. They did not bring with them contemporary currents in English architecture but the timeless standards of the countryside. As the economy grew and New England became more cosmopolitan, the simple colonial style quickly gave way to the grander style known as Georgian, a development that parallels the region's move away from the sacred toward the secular.

The early settlers of New England built their homes of sturdy oak, as had been the custom in rural England. Even though oak was a seemingly inexhaustible resource in the New World, the

BELOW: **Built in 1664 and restored in 1934, the Whitman House is considered a classic specimen of the New England colonial style. Its small windows, jutting front façade, and gabled overhang illustrate some of the asymmetrical oddities of early colonialism.** *Whitman House, Farmington, Connecticut*

ABOVE: **Except for the central gabled window added by Samuel Ripley in 1845, Concord's legendary Old Manse has hardly changed since it was built by William Emerson in 1770.** *The Old Manse, Concord, Massachusetts*

settlers quickly adopted a system of oak rationing, remembering its scarcity back in England. Heavy oak frames, held together by mortise and tenon joints, were raised by joiners and carpenters and reinforced with various kinds of braces and girts. Meshes of wattle and daub—sticks and clay or lime—were used for insulation.

Most early house plans incorporated two rooms, one slightly larger than the other, around a massive central chimney—the most distinctive feature

of the early New England home. By the late seventeenth century, a lean-to in the back, usually the site of the kitchen, was a common addition. The two ground-floor rooms were called the hall and the parlor. also known as the best room, the parlor served multiple functions. As the main entertaining room, it housed the best and most ornamental furniture in the house. In a surprising custom that did not change until well into the eighteenth century, the parlor also served as the bedroom of the

LEFT: Nathaniel Hawthorne's bedroom in the Old Manse. One of the greatest of all New England writers, Hawthorne lived in the Old Manse and immortalized it in his famous novel, *Mosses From an Old Manse. The Old Manse, Concord, Massachusetts*

LEFT: The dining room of the Old Manse. Nathanial Hawthorne was not the Old Manse's only literary resident. Ralph Waldo Emerson inhabited the venerable house in the 1830s and wrote frequently of the splendor of the house and its surroundings. *The Old Manse, Concord, Massachusetts*

RIGHT: Built in 1710, The Nims is one of the many fine Colonial structures still existing today in Deerfield Village in the Connecticut River Valley, a gold mine of early American heritage. *The Nims House, Old Deerfield Village, Massachusetts*

parents of the household. The hall was a more practical working space; food was prepared there and guests put up for the night. The corresponding upstairs rooms served as sleeping quarters for children and as storage space.

By the early eighteenth century, a more spacious and refined four-room plan had gained in popularity. This development was accompanied by an increasing interest in interior aesthetics. Plaster, trims, and moldings began to cover the structural elements that were once left exposed. High ceilings and larger windows reflected the new expansiveness of the culture. The new buildings also made a structural distinction between formal and casual; there were now two parlors, one serving as the traditional best room, the other commonly used for casual gatherings.

As there were no old buildings to inhabit or repair, houses sprung up rapidly in the early days of New England, and skilled carpenters were in great demand. Many English carpenters, recognizing that the urgent need of skilled builders meant big money, came over to fill the void and outraged the likes of Governor Winthrop with their exorbitant rates. Opportunistic craftsmen brought with

them trends in English architecture and trades, an influx of tools and techniques that would transform the New England home.

In the early days of New England, craftsmen and artisans were, by necessity, jacks of all trades. As time passed, specialization increased, in part as a result of a great migration of artisans, many of whom were excluded from the traditional craft guilds in England. In general, the furniture of early New England is characterized by the aesthetic of functionality. Craftsmen were in short supply and the multifarious demands of starting a New World did not allow people to lavish time and money on fineries.

Even so, it is a mistake to think that Puritans eschewed fashion and ornament for religious reasons. Quite to the contrary, the furniture designs favored by the Puritans were of the Italian mannerist style, a style known for its "exaggerated proportions" and "grotesque ornament," according to one scholar. In England, mannerism had become associated specifically with Puritanism, an identifying, fraternal style. Naturally, this knowledge and preference crossed the ocean with the Puritans.

FOLLOWING PAGE: The historic Eleazer Arnold house, built in 1687, boldly displays several defining characteristics of the New England colonial style, especially the massive chimney. Arnold, an amateur architect of sorts, enjoyed unadorned natural materials, following the medieval ideal. The Arnold House was raised from one to two stories in 1800. *The Eleazer Arnold House, Lincoln, Rhode Island*

LEFT: The Dwight-Barnard House, yet another fine specimen of colonial architecture to be found in old Deerfield Village, provides a particularly good example of the popular colonial gambrel roof. *Dwight-Barnard House, Deerfield, Massachusetts*

GEORGIAN HOUSES OF NEW ENGLAND

A new kind of settler—educated, worldly, urban, and, at least by the standards of the original settlers, wealthy—began arriving in America in the late seventeenth and early eighteenth centuries. Predictably, the new immigrants exerted a profound influence over the appearance of colonial New England. If the homes of the original settlers expressed the rigors of the frontier, the homes of the new class of voyagers would express the great riches to be mined there. They had come from cities; they had toured "the Continent;" they were current and conversant in the language and traditions of architecture. In America, they sought not sanctuary in the wilderness but the seemingly unlimited space and resources. As Hugh Morrison wrote in *Early American Architecture*:

If Parson Capen had to stoop to enter his low-beamed rooms, it was merely becoming to one whose cares were spiritual, and if his wife appeared a little awkward climbing down the steep and torturous stair, no harm was done. But a few miles away and fifty years later, Issac Royall needed a room befitting his name for the expansive and graceful gestures of the minuet, and a wide and easy flight of steps for the gracious descent of a wife who brought her own twenty-seven slaves from Antigua.

Thus, around 1700, the colonial style gave way to the Georgian in New England, and, in fact, in most regions of early America. The former had been a reflection of the medieval styles favored by simple country folk in England, the latter an interpretation of the Italian Renaissance styles that had

LEFT: The Ropes Mansion was the home of Judge Nathaniel Ropes, a British Loyalist who was literally besieged there in 1774 by a mob of angry Patriots. The Loyalists were strongest in the far southern colonies—Georgia and the Carolinas—and in Middle Atlantic colonies such as New York and Pennsylvania. *Ropes Mansion, Salem, Massachusetts*

LEFT: Newport is known for its many fine Georgian public buildings, often the work of the great architect Peter Harrison, as well as for the Hunter House, an excellent Georgian specimen famous for its balustrade roof. *Hunter House, Newport, Rhode Island*

been popular among the English elite since the early part of the seventeenth century. English designers such as Inigo Jones had brought Renaissance classicism to England, the rules of classical architecture as expounded by the Roman Vitruvius in the first century B.C. and adapted in the sixteenth century by the Italian Andrea Palladio. Christopher Wren, considered by many the greatest of all English architects, virtually rebuilt London in the Renaissance image after the great fire of 1666.

The Georgian style first spread to the New England coastal towns and cities—where business was booming with the highest concentration of shippers and traders—and was first expressed in the form of large and grand public buildings. Since the Georgian was at first a style associated with opulence, the best examples of early Georgian homes in New England are mansions and estates. But New England, unlike the South, gave rise to a middle class and the resultant scaled-down middle-class Georgian house to be found frequently in Boston and other bustling cultural centers.

Georgian homes are defined by their formality and regularity. Their symmetrical, geometric shapes were a marked contrast to the irregularity of colonial structures (houses that were frequently expanded and modified, thus shaped by accident and necessity). Everything about the Georgian house, from its windows to its doorways, was rhythmic. Doorways were flanked by columns and topped with cornices. Windows were generally of the sliding-sash variety and grew bigger and more elaborate as the Georgian period progressed.

One of the most significant features of the Georgian period was a new attention to exterior treatments, a dramatic departure from the simple timber houses of the colonial period. In New England, brick masonry became popular, as did the use of graduated clapboard—wide shingles on the bottom diminishing as they ascend to amplify the illusion of height. The Georgian roof tended to be considerably less slanted than the colonial, often times flattening out on top into a kind of roof deck. Dormer windows were another common feature of the Georgian roof.

Inside, the Georgian house abounded with details—elaborate mantelpieces, paneled surfaces, and window treatments. Ceilings were higher than the colonial predecessors, stairways

BELOW: **The grandest house on Brattle Street in Cambridge, the Long-fellow House was originally known as the Vassall House, after Major John Vassall who built the house in 1759. Henry Wadsworth Longfellow lived there from 1837 until his death in 1882. Though the interior of the house has been preserved to reflect Longfellow's era, the exterior remains of the classic late Georgian style.** *Longfellow House, Cambridge, Massachusetts*

RIGHT: **The Hunter House was built in 1746, the pinnacle of the Georgian years in New England, before the renaissance Georgian style gave way to what would become known as the Federal style.** *Hunter House, Newport, Rhode Island*

HUNTER HOUSE
Built 1746
HEADQUARTERS of ADMIRAL De TERNAY
OF THE FRENCH FLEET
1780 - 1781

RIGHT: Like Deerfield, Massachusetts, Wethersfield, Connecticut, is another rich repository of preserved colonial-era homes. This one, the Isaac Stevens House, is actually subdued Georgian in style. *Isaac Stevens House, Wethersfield, Connecticut*

RIGHT: With its large central chimney, this house in Wethersfield, Connecticut, serves as a fairly typical example of the colonial saltbox style. It was probably built in the early eighteenth century. *Wethersfield, Connecticut*

wider and of a more gradual ascent. Decorative carving adorned handrails, steps, and floors. And, in perhaps the most significant departure from the colonial period, Georgian houses were veritable museums of fine and functional art: furniture in the Queen Anne and Chippendale styles, tea tables, needlework rugs, family portraits, fine paintings, and prints.

If the colonial style was, in essence, an anti-style, an outgrowth of plain necessity, then as the first major development in New England architecture, the Georgian was not new at all. It was simply a matter of the New World catching up to the tastes and fashions that had prevailed in England for the better part of a century. The new breed of settlers, however, imported more than just styles and skills; with them also came the class distinctions and social strata that the original settlers had sought to escape. Thus, the colonial and Georgian styles co-existed in New England, one reflecting the humble origins of the original settlers, the other the breeding and education of the merchants who followed. There are more surviving colonial structures in New England than in any other region of America. The area stands as a living testament to the conflicting forces— the modesty and the pretension, austerity and wealth—of colonial America.

BELOW: **Like the Old Manse in Concord, Salem's House of the Seven Gables was immortalized by Nathanial Hawthorne. Originally known as the Turner House, Seven Gables is a dazzlingly complex rambling Gothic structure that has been rebuilt and modified countless times since its original construction in 1670.**
The House of Seven Gables, Salem, Massachusetts

CHAPTER TWO

THE MIDDLE COLONIES

From the very beginning, the middle colonies of early America, and especially New York, were more heterogeneous, inclusive, and boisterous than Puritan New England. Commerce, not religion, was the magnet that drew the settlers across the ocean. Although not always serene, an atmosphere of tolerance bordering on anarchy prevailed in the middle colonies, allowing New York and its surroundings to become America's first melting pot—a raucous brew of Dutch, English, Swedish, and German settlers living and trading, for the most part peaceably, among the native tribes.

In Pennsylvania and New Jersey, the Quakers—those misunderstood and often despised religious radicals—found the space in which they could live relatively unbothered. William Penn imagined that the city he created virtually by himself, Philadelphia, would serve as a haven and a refuge for the persecuted. He approached the natives in friendship and encouraged oft-harassed religious sects, such as the German Pietists, to settle anew in the tolerant and open environment of his "Holy Experiment."

Thus, between the "rough and unrestrained" Dutch settlements and Penn's Quaker utopia, the

BELOW: The Wright's Ferry Mansion, built in 1738, typifies the Quaker interpretation of the emergent Georgian style. Although the house was designed by and for English Quakers, the red oak shingles suggest that local German craftsmen were probably involved in the construction. *Wright's Ferry Mansion, Columbia, Pennsylvania*

LEFT: The Hampton National Historic Site was acquired by the National Park Service in 1948 for its outstanding historical and architectural merits. Built by Charles Ridgely between 1783 and 1790, the house today rests on 60 acres of grounds that include outbuildings and formal gardens. *Hampton National Historic Site, Maryland*

BELOW: **Even after the English seized New Amsterdam in 1664, Dutch families and customs continued to thrive in the region for years to come. The Philipsburgh Manor is one the great existing examples of an early Dutch estate along the Hudson River.** *Philipsburgh Manor, North Tarrytown, New York*

middle colonies offered a mix of culture in striking contrast to the relative uniformity of New England. It is not surprising, then, that the architecture and art of the region reflect a rich blend of influences and trends marked by much dialogue and cross-breeding. If New England stands for the religiously radical origins of America, and the South for the persistence of aristocracy, then the middle colonies reflect the open, industrious, expansive, and inclusive spirit of early America.

THE DUTCH IN EARLY AMERICA

Just as the *Mayflower* "missed" northern Virginia and happened instead on New England, so did the Dutch colonial settlements begin as something of an accident. English-born explorer Henry Hudson was hired by the Dutch East India Company to find a quick and convenient passage to the East. He found instead the river and valley that now bear his name. Hudson reported back that the fertile region seemed well suited to the fur and farming trades. Soon thereafter, the Dutch East India Company became the Dutch West India Company. Dutch settlers were not driven from their homeland, as were the Puritans, but drawn across the ocean by the prospect of money to be made and resources to be exploited. New Netherland quickly acquired a more international character than neighboring New England. Many people of a variety of nationalities and religions were interested in making money and invested in the venture. Cultural and religious uniformity were secondary, although the resultant diversity frequently led to squabbling over territories and rights.

RIGHT: **This is the Dining Room of Hampton, a late Georgian-style mansion notable for its aristocratic atmosphere. It is said that the silver on the table was a gift from Lafayette, the French general and political leader who joined George Washington's army during the Revolutionary War.** *Hampton National Historic Site, Maryland*

The fur trade necessitated good relations with the Indians, a practice of consideration and respect that began when Hudson himself took several Iroquois leaders aboard his vessel and got at least one of them drunk on wine. Later, when Peter Minuit arrived to direct the New Netherland colony, he was instructed that:

> In case there should be Indians living on the aforesaid island of Manhattan or claiming any title to it, as also to other places that might suit our purpose, they must not be expelled with violence or threats, but be persuaded with kind words (to let us settle there), or otherwise should be given something for it to placate them. . .

Minuit purchased the island for the now-famous sum of twenty-four dollars (sixty guilders).

Manhattan island quickly grew into a little Amsterdam with curved lanes, gabled roofs—the prototype of the famed Manhattan skyline—and rich and fertile farms and orchards surrounding the city. The robust little city drew a plethora of artisans and craftsmen from Europe. There were no exclusive guilds here, and there was plenty of work to be done. Interestingly, Manhattan's residents had already developed a reputation as a coarse and unrefined sort, uneducated and obsessed with profit, at least in the eyes of Boston. This may well reflect deeper tensions between the English and the Dutch, no small part of which were disputes over which country the area that is now New York rightly belonged to.

Despite the vitality and diversity of New Amsterdam—as early as 1643, as many as eighteen different languages were spoken there—Dutch settlement in New York simply did not take hold for a variety of reasons. The Dutch were not nearly as enthusiastic about colonization as the English. The Dutch West India Company's attempts to encourage colonization, including the ill-fated Patroon system, were generally dismal failures. Patroons were offered large chunks of land and remittance from taxes under the condition they populate the "patroonship" within a four year period. By the 1660s, the ownership of all of the patroonships in New Netherland had reverted back to the Dutch West India Company.

In 1664, the English swept up the Hudson River and took command of the struggling Dutch territories. The Dutch settlers, long unhappy with the arbitrary and somewhat tyrannical rule of Governor Peter Stuyvesant and the Dutch West India Company, welcomed the generous conditions of English rule and offered little resistance. New Netherland had hardly lasted twenty-five years as a fledgling colony, but in the style and architecture of Manhattan, and in the pockets of Dutch culture along the Hudson, the Dutch influence on New York has endured.

DUTCH HOMES IN NEW YORK

The early Dutch settlers faced conditions similar to those encountered by their New England counterparts: an often harsh climate, a surplus of wood, and a dearth of skilled builders. It is no surprise, then, that their first dwellings bore a resemblance to the timber framed houses of New England. As more and more people arrived in the 1620s and '30s, however, the Dutch style began to assert itself. The Dutch burghers of New Amsterdam and the Fort Orange region (now Albany) expressed their nationalistic spirit in brick, the most popular of all building materials in Holland. The farming communities of the Hudson Valley

LEFT: Settled in 1678 by the Huguenots, the town of New Paltz features several fine examples of early Dutch Colonial architecture. The thick walls were built of native stone. Inside, the earliest, unmodified Huguenot houses generally adhered to modest one-room floor plans. *Abraham Hasbrouck House, New Paltz, New York*

and New Jersey are best known for their stone houses. The unique flared-eaves homes of Long Island, once thought to be the first genuine specimen of a new and native colonial style, have since been identified as Flemish in origin. In architecture, as in culture, the middle colonies were defined by diversity.

According to early descriptions, New Amsterdam was an accurate miniature of its namesake. All the defining features of the Dutch city—curved streets, canals, gardens, plentiful taverns, and even windmills—could be found there. Houses were of brick and two and a half to three stories high. The most obvious and distinct features were the gabled roofs and ornate transom windows. Manhattan retained its primarily Dutch appearance well into the eighteenth century, even though by then it had long been under English rule and had truly become a cosmopolitan melting pot.

Unfortunately, many of the city's original structures were destroyed by the fire of 1776, and most of those that did survive soon fell in the wake of commerce and growth. Still, the strong Dutch character of New York City is especially apparent in lower Manhattan, the present-day financial district.

The best examples of early Dutch colonial houses survive, in plenitude, in the towns along the Hudson north of Manhattan. The famous stone houses of the mid-Hudson Valley have become virtually synonymous with Dutch colonial, although it is worth noting that their builders, given the resources and leisure, would have preferred homes of brick. Stones of irregular size and contour were picked from the fields or broken off of ledges. The original mortar used was a makeshift concoction of clay bound with straw or hair. Soon, lime became available locally and the

RIGHT: The Morris-Jumel Mansion's elaborate formal dining room was largely the work of Eliza Bowen, Stephen Jumel's wife, the daughter of a poor Rhode Island family who became one of the wealthiest women in New York. Eliza Bowen later married Aaron Burr. *Morris-Jumel Mansion, New York, New York*

ABOVE: New York's famous Morris-Jumel Mansion on the Harlem River was built by Roger Morris in 1765 and bought by Stephen Jumel in 1810. When the British forces withdrew from Manhattan in 1776, the house briefly served as General George Washington's headquarters. *Morris-Jumel Mansion, New York, New York*

FOLLOWING PAGE: One of several fine Georgian houses in Odessa, the William Corbit House echoes the architectural styles that reigned in nearby Philadelphia—including the fine brick masonry, abundant windows, and arched doorway. *William Corbit House, Odessa, Delaware*

with the peculiar projecting or "flying" gutters. Early historians, in the absence of a sound historical explanation, were left to conclude that these structures represented the first authentic and new American house, the first architectural style in the New World without a clear antecedent in the Old. Twentieth-century investigators, however, have now convincingly identified the style as Flemish, the product of the Flemings and Walloons who had emigrated with the Dutch in the 1620s. It would take considerably longer for a distinctly American style of architecture to emerge.

ABOVE: Not to be mistaken with the Van Cortlandt House in New York City, Croton-on-Hudson's Van Cortlandt Manor was built in the late seventeenth century and substantially remodeled in 1749. This house was the center of an enormous and industrious estate owned by the prosperous Van Cortlandt family. *Van Cortlandt Manor, Croton-on-Hudson, New York*

lime-based mortar increased the durability and stability of the homes. The imposing walls, sometimes as much as 3 feet thick, framed narrow floor plans. The typical early Hudson Valley home was only one room deep, with three rooms strung along the length of the house. Because of their rough-hewn exterior and relatively small size, early Dutch colonial houses appear modest and rustic. As time progressed and the region enjoyed an influx of artisans and craftsmen, the styles and tastes of the Dutch settlers expanded, mirroring the growth of the Georgian in New England. Although few survive today, the manors of the Albany region rival the great Georgian houses of Virginia.

Architectural historians were long puzzled by the style of house that prevailed on Long Island, southern New York, and portions of northern New Jersey. These houses, though apparently built by the Dutch and of the same period as the houses of New Amsterdam and the Hudson Valley, display markedly different and unique features, most notably the sloping gambrel roofs

THE QUAKERS IN PENNSYLVANIA
Aristocrat, idealist, and unlikely Quaker, William Penn was almost single-handedly responsible for the settling of the Delaware Valley and the founding of Philadelphia. Penn was a member of the English elite by birth. His Quakerism stemmed from his association with the founder of the Society of Friends, George Fox, a relationship that Penn's family and friends frowned on. Quakerism (the word was actually a popular term of derision) was thought by most Anglicans to be bothersome at best, heretical at worst. The Quaker notion that spirituality was a highly personal matter to be kept separate from politics and government implicitly threatened the core premise of Anglicanism. But Penn was an iconoclast of the first order, a paradoxical combination of worldly connections and Utopian idealism. Quakers were despised and persecuted in England, as they would be in regions of America as well. It was Penn's efforts to establish

an American haven for Quakers that lead to the most tolerant, open-minded, and progressive settlement in the New World:

> You will be governed by laws of your own making, and live a free, and, if you will, a sober and industrious people.

The first destination of Quakers in America was New Jersey, or rather the Jerseys: East and West. Numerous parties claimed dominion in the Jerseys, an impossibly complicated and controversial chaos of rights and territories. Such political volatility did not provide the ideal environment

for the safe and tolerant haven Penn envisioned. Penn petitioned King Charles II for the rights to a stretch of land between New York and Maryland. When Penn was granted his charter in 1681, he began to design—literally—his "Holy Experiment," the city of brotherly love. Penn forthwith sent a letter to the local Indians, expressing his respect and his willingness to work out satisfactory and mutually beneficial treaties.

Penn's grand vision encouraged a great swarm of people to resettle in Philadelphia. In fact, Penn himself frequently traveled back to Europe to appeal to the harassed and persecuted. By the 1690s, Philadelphia had become the third largest

BELOW: **Anticipating the city-like sprawl of the later Georgian estates, Van Cortlandt Manor features many interesting outbuildings such as this ferry house. The Van Cortlandt family owned and occupied the estate for nearly 250 years.** *The Ferry House at Van Cortlandt Manor, Croton-on-Hudson, New York*

city on the eastern seaboard. People were drawn by both the cultural climate of openness and opportunity and by the literal climate, the varied but relatively mild seasons, the deep harbor of the Delaware, and the great fertility of the surrounding farmlands. To accommodate the settlers, Penn himself designed the plans for a 12,000-acre city—far larger than most cities at the time—and an orderly arrangement and system of distributing lots. Penn's symmetrical grid featured wide thoroughfares and copious land set aside for parks and commons. The city was surrounded on every side by rich farmlands populated by "gentlemen farmers."

Philadelphia soon developed varied and productive industries. It became a major exporter of wheat, meat, timber, and natural minerals. As the city prospered more and more, it became less a Quaker haven and more a magnet for merchants

of all kinds. Penn's principles of acceptance and peaceful cohabitation survived, even if the quiet austerity of the Quakers gave way to a bustling commercial environment. By the mid-eighteenth century, Quakers comprised barely one-sixth the population of Philadelphia. The shipbuilding, blacksmithing, and foundry industries thrived and the appearance of the city underwent continual transformation. Cobblestone streets replaced the dirt lanes of old. Fortunately, Penn's expansive city grid accommodated such feverish growth, protecting Philadelphia from the chaos that would have befallen most other cities in the face of wild and uncontrollable expansion. More than any other colonial city, Philadelphia succeeded in distancing itself from Europe and establishing a truly American spirit. It was a hub of political activity as well as enterprising and innovative business, the avant-garde of revolutionary thinking.

RIGHT: **The stone exterior of the Wright's Ferry Mansion is fairly typical of early Pennsylvanian architecture. The stark, untreated floors and windows reflect the austerity of Quaker living.** *Wright's Ferry Mansion, Columbia, Pennsylvania*

LEFT: **This sandy limestone house was built by Hans Herr in 1719, and constructed almost entirely from materials found on the property. Such thick-walled limestone houses were quite common in the heavily-Germanic areas of Pennsylvania, but the Hans Herr House is one of very few still standing today.** *Hans Herr House, Lancaster, Pennsylvania*

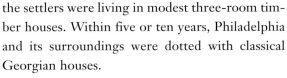

THE HOUSES OF PENNSYLVANIA

Because Pennsylvania was the latest of all the early colonial settlements, it virtually bypassed the true colonial stage of architecture. When the Quakers arrived in great numbers in the 1680s and '90s, they brought with them the currents of English urban architecture: namely, the Renaissance-influenced Georgian style. True, the original settlers of Philadelphia, as all original settlers, lived in rugged pioneer conditions, in this case in crude dugouts and caves along the banks of the Delaware River. Within several years, however,

the settlers were living in modest three-room timber houses. Within five or ten years, Philadelphia and its surroundings were dotted with classical Georgian houses.

This accelerated architectural evolution can be explained in several ways. First, Penn's plot of land was extraordinarily rich in natural resources, and the climate was mild enough to permit year-round building. Secondly, Penn's policy of tolerance and inclusivity drew swarms of people from many different cultures, each bringing their own technologies and sensibilities. Finally, the inroads made by earlier settlers from New England and the South relieved the Pennsylvanians of many of the burdens of starting anew.

The first formal neighborhoods of Philadelphia featured three-story brick houses arranged row-style, a direct reflection of the prevailing tastes in London. For these settlers, unlike those in New England and New York, ample clay and limestone made bricks readily available. These houses exhibited the classical symmetry and regularity of the Georgian style, but were generally without an abundance of ornate detail. Penn himself was rumored to have lived in a fairly typical house on Letitia Street, a somewhat plain brick residence with all the earmarks of the early Georgian—regularly-spaced sliding sash windows, paneled shutters, and dormer windows.

As Philadelphia was essentially a planned city, it took its architecture very seriously. By the early eighteenth century, Penn had attracted all variety of carpenters, tradesmen, bricklayers, and masons and established America's first builders' guild. They assembled an architectural library, distributed pamphlets on better building, and were generally of service to anyone in need of assistance in the design or construction of a house. In 1771, the builders' guild built its own meeting hall on Chestnut Street. It was an attempt at a higher classical style, featuring a crowning cupola, pedimented doorways, and arched windows. Whether the building was architecturally significant is moot. In 1774, it earned its immortality as the meeting place of the First Continental Congress.

A distinct regional style also took shape in the country houses of the farming lands outside of Philadelphia and in Delaware, Maryland, and the southern counties of New Jersey. Depending on availability, the homes of the wealthier gentlemen farmers were built of either stone or brick. Stone façades were sometimes covered in a coat of stucco. Many brick houses exhibited elaborate brick patterns—zigzags, diamonds, and checkerboards.

It is a widely acknowledged truth that, as time passed, regional differences lessened in the colonies and, consciously or not, Americans—at least the wealthy ones—moved toward a national style. That style, evident in the famous mansions of New England, the middle colonies, and the South, was the late Georgian. There are, of course, fascinating exceptions to this rule, pockets of

cultural homogeneity in which a traditional style persists in the face of sweeping trends. One of the most famous of these styles is the Pennsylvania Dutch, the architectural counterpart of the dialect of the same name. The Pennsylvania Dutch were, or course, Germans who had emigrated from the Rhine Valley region of Germany at the encouragement of William Penn himself. They came in great numbers and brought with them unique and distinct architectural styles and crafts. They are perhaps best known for stout hewn-log houses and barns, a visual treat for tourists to this day in York and Lancaster Counties, among other parts of the region. If Penn's Philadelphia represents a dynamic fusion of cultures, the Pennsylvania Dutch provide a reminder that diversity does not necessarily require blending in.

ABOVE: Bartram's house is significant in that it displays some of the characteristics of Swedish architecture, a style of design that predates William Penn's influence on Pennsylvanian houses. The house is otherwise distinguished by its gardens. Bartram is generally considered to be the first American botanist. *John Bartram's House, Philadelphia Pennsylvania*

CHAPTER THREE

THE SOUTH

And Cheerfully at Sea,
Successe you will intice,
To get the Pearles and Gold,
And ours to hold,
Virginia
Earth's onely Paradise

Where nature hath in store
Fowl, venison and fish,
And the Fruitfulls't soil
Without your toil Three harvests more,
All greater than you wish.

    —MICHAEL DRAYTON, *TO THE VIRGINIA VOYAGE*

In popular travel litera-
ture, verse, and the propaganda and promotions
distributed by the Virginia Company, Virginia was
portrayed as a paradise in climate, resource, and
opportunity. In truth, little was known of the
territory, the natives who lived there, and the real
challenges and dangers that settlers would
encounter. But the image of paradise lured a
sizable band of settlers, mostly gentlemen adventurers with a seriously misguided notion of what
life would be like there.

The early English settlements of the southern
portion of the American East Coast would be
marked by recurrent tragedies, death by starvation, disease, and attack, interminable in-fighting
and poor organization, and, finally, triumph by
sheer persistence. In all respects the colonial South
was characterized by extremes. In time, the richest
colonists would live there alongside the poorest,
the gracious and stunning Georgian manors of the
wealthy farm owners offset by dingy mud and
wattle dwellings of enslaved farm workers. Some
might argue that the dichotomies of southern life,
initiated in the first years of settlement, persist
until this day.

LEFT: Shirley, built by
Charles Carter, owes a
heavy debt to the influence
of Palladianism—the influence of renaissance architect Andrea Palladio—as
can be seen in the two-story
classic porticoes. Shirley
bears a strong resemblance
to the Palladian Capitol of
Williamsburg, Virginia, which,
some suggest, may have been
designed in part by Thomas
Jefferson. *Shirley, Charles
City, Virginia*

LEFT: Recreated slave
cabins at Carter's Grove.
Carter's Grove, as with
so many of the south's
great estates, was built
on the tobacco and slave
industries. More than
any other documentary
evidence, southern
mansions illustrate
this striking dichotomy
between extremely
rich and extremely
poor. *Carter's Grove,
Williamsburg, Virginia*

THE JAMESTOWN SETTLEMENT

The history of Jamestown, the first lasting English settlement in America, is not a pleasant one. Rarely, if ever, have would-be pioneers been so misguided and ill-informed in their undertaking, and rarely have they suffered so much. Gold, that perpetual metaphor for the promise of America, was the lure. The original settlers of Jamestown, those aboard the *Sarah Constant*, the *Goodspeed*, and the *Discovery*, were enticed by reports of gold in the hills of Virginia. As if to veil the voyage in sober-minded respectability, however, the Virginia Charter of 1606 claimed the spreading of Christianity among "the Infidels and Savages, living in those Parts" as its mission.

Under the command of Captain Christopher Newport, the expedition arrived at the newly christened Point Comfort in April of 1607 after a difficult and tumultuous passage. To the sea-weary travelers, many of whom were aristocrats, any land looked like good land, even the low-lying and mosquito-ridden Jamestown Peninsula. In retrospect, the choice of settlements could not have been less propitious. Jamestown Peninsula was isolated, swampy, and surrounded by Indians. Within one year of their arrival, all but thirty-eight of the one hundred and four adventurers had succumbed to starvation, disease, or Native American attacks. And the situation would deteriorate before it improved.

First-person accounts of the Jamestown settlement cite poor organization and preparation as the root causes of the early difficulty. The settlers—money-motivated employees and stockholders of the Virginia Company—were less interested in the mundane and necessary duties of developing a sturdy settlement than in the discovery of gold.

RIGHT: Considered one of the finest of the eighteenth-century plantation houses, Kenmore was built by Fielding Lewis, husband of George Washington's sister Betty, between 1752 and 1756. Kenmore is situated on 863 acres by the Rappahannock River. *Kenmore, Fredericksburg, Virginia*

LEFT: The blue bedchamber at Kenmore. During the Revolutionary War, Fielding Lewis managed his own estate at Kenmore as well as the properties of his brother-in-law George Washington. Kenmore had made his fortunes in the tobacco trade, but lost much of his wealth as a result of the war's effect on the currency and economy of Virginia. *Kenmore, Fredericksburg, Virginia*

RIGHT: The famous fine plasterwork featured in Kenmore's formal dining room was done, according to Fielding Lewis, by a "Frenchman." *Kenmore, Fredericksburg, Virginia*

LEFT: The modest and functional slaves' kitchen and work area inside Carter's Grove mansion starkly contrasts with the grandeur and decorative detail found elsewhere in the mansion. Though not ornate, the fine flooring and panelled doors are notable. *Carter's Grove, Williamsburg, Virginia*

RIGHT: Among the many masterpieces at Carter's Grove are its gardens, including the famous Circular Garden, which, like so much of Virginia, borrows heavily from English traditions. *Carter's Grove, Williamsburg, Virginia*

LEFT: The spectacular mansion at Carter's Grove stands about 6 miles south of Williamsburg, Virginia, just north of the James River. It was built by Carter Burwell between 1750 and 1753 and designed, it is presumed, by the great Georgian architect Richard Taliaferro. *Carter's Grove Mansion, Williamsburg, Virginia*

ABOVE: **Ornate detail abounds at Kenmore, even in the Kitchen House and the many other outbuildings. As Fielding Lewis grew wealthier (in part because of his marriage to Betty Washington) his Kenmore estate naturally grew more lavish.** *The Kitchen House at Kenmore, Fredericksburg, Virginia*

The settlers were factious and mutinous. By 1608, they had already executed several of their own and imprisoned many others, including Captain John Smith. In fact, Smith was imprisoned and awaiting execution when the settlement's governor was ousted and Smith named his successor. Throughout the early years of the settlement, the planting of crops and building of fortifications were half-hearted and shoddy. For basic supplies, the settlement was entirely dependent upon ships arriving from England. The unpredictability of sea travel caused many dire shortages of food, seed, and building materials.

The Jamestown settlement owes its survival to the stern rule of Captain John Smith, who, in 1608, took command, enforced discipline, and, insofar as it was possible, cured the Jamestown settlers of their gold lust. In Smith's year as leader—a decisive year in the history of Virginia—twenty houses were built, corn was sown, livestock raised, and relatively favorable relations established with some, though hardly all,

of the local Indians. By no means did this signify the beginning of smooth sailing. In fact, Smith left Jamestown for the last time in 1609. Subsequent leaders had difficulty matching his successful if dictatorial rule. Disorder, dissension, and an almost unthinkable mortality rate continued to plague the settlement. In the period between 1609 and 1611, popularly known as the "starving time," the population of Jamestown fell from five hundred to sixty.

When Sir Thomas Gates arrived in Jamestown in 1611, he found a weak, sick, and psychologically damaged population. Malaria, bad water, famine, and attacks by Native Americans(the worst of which were yet to come) had ravaged the settlement:

> If there were any conscience in men, it would make their harts to bleede to heare the pittiful murmurings and outcries of our sick men without reliefe. . . some departing out of the World, many times three or foure in a night, in the morning their bodies trailed out of cabines like Dogges to be buried.

Gates saw no hope for the settlement. His employer, the Virginia Company, was angered by the disappointing returns of the venture, a trend that would lead eventually to the company's collapse. In an act of mercy, Gates rounded up the dispirited survivors and headed back for England in 1610, only to be met at the mouth of the James River by three English ships stocked with fresh men and abundant supplies.

FOLLOWING PAGE:
Located 25 miles north of Williamsburg, Westover is perhaps the most famous Georgian mansion in America. Westover belonged to the wealthy and prominent Virginian William Byrd II, a sportsman and politician who held many public offices. *Westover, Westover, Virginia*

LEFT: A sculpture of Pan graces the gardens at Brandon. Georgianism was, after all, grounded in a deep appreciation for all things classical. Thus, classical sculptures such as this one of the Greek god Pan were a common and popular ornament among the wealthy and cultured. *Brandon, Prince George County, Virginia*

Gates and his men were convinced to return to Jamestown.

The man who did the convincing, Lord Delaware, served as governor of Virginia from 1610 to 1618. The rule of Lord Delaware and his deputy governors, Gates and Sir Thomas Dale, brought stability, discipline, and, in time, prosperity to Virginia. To provide sorely needed incentive, the firm-handed Dale abolished the communal plantation system, as Bradford would later do in New England, and allotted 3 acres of land to about eighty of the more enterprising and energetic settlers. Dale imposed a kind of martial law, considered extreme by some but effective in establishing order and purpose in the notoriously disorganized colony. Although the colony steadily progressed toward stability, there would be continued setbacks. So long as there was no basis for a prosperous economy, subsistence and survival would be the best the Jamestown settlers could hope for.

The original settlers had felt quite sure that gold would be their fortune in Virginia. In fact, it was tobacco. Tobacco had become highly popular in England, often touted as a cure for virtually every kind of ailment. Exporting tobacco provided the Virginians with the reliable cash crop they needed to get on firm footing. Once the Virginians had discovered the value of the home-

ly weed, they sowed it everywhere, along streets and in front yards. It had become so lucrative and appealing that Dale actually had to force the settlers to plant at least two other crops, preferably edible ones. Thus did tobacco become the cornerstone of the South's economy, the origin of the large southern plantations, and the discovery that safely established Virginia as America's first lasting colony.

EARLY COLONIAL HOUSES IN THE SOUTH

Jamestown, Charleston, Maryland, Georgia: As the names of southern cities and states suggests, the settlers of the South were devoted English people, loyal to the crown. They felt no opposition to the Anglican Church. They represented a wide spectrum of the English social classes—from

LEFT: In 1929, the Robert E. Lee Memorial Foundation purchased Stratford and saw to the renovation of its interiors, including the restoration of furnishings and the return to original colors of the rooms. *Stratford, Stratford, Virginia*

RIGHT: Thomas Lee, Governor of Virginia, built Stratford on his 16,000 acre plantation. Construction took place between 1725 and 1730, making this one of the early great Georgian mansions of Virginia. The enclosed, balustraded roof decks, it is said, allowed Lee to view his ships on the Potomac River. *Stratford, Stratford, Virginia*

LEFT: In 1765, Brandon was built for Nathanial Harrison, it is believed, by a twenty-two year old Thomas Jefferson, the best man at Harrison's wedding. Jefferson, if he in fact did design it, borrowed the plan from Robert Morris's book *Select Architecture*, a little known text that Jefferson admired immensely. *Brandon, Prince George County, Virginia*

ABOVE: **Built around 1765 by Charles Moore on a royal land grant, Walnut Grove Plantation gets its name from the walnut trees planted by Moore's daughter, Kate Moore Barry, around 1800.** *Walnut Grove Plantation, Spartanburg, South Carolina*

squires and merchants to artisans and indentured servants. The South, more than other colonial regions, was also geared more toward the ocean, dependent from the very beginning on exportation and importation. Thus in art, fashion, and architecture, its ties to the mother country were fluid and strong. Colonization represented an extension of, not a traumatic break from, the traditions of England.

In culture and architecture, the South would eventually mimic the sharp class stratification of Europe. In a sense, it was more of a "new England" than the colony that bore that name. It would give rise to a wealthy agricultural aristocracy and produce some of the most dazzling plantation mansions on the continent. But, as the nearly catastrophic Jamestown experience ensured, the rise from a shaky and perpetually endangered

settlement to an established and highly cultured society took a long time. Perhaps even more than New England and the middle colonies, the early architecture of the South reflects the functionality born of precarious conditions and hostile environment.

Though only fragments remain of the Jamestown settlement, scholars believe that three different kinds of houses were built there: hewn-timber frame houses, invariably the first kind of permanent structure in heavily forested frontiers; brick houses, apparently appearing as early as 1611; and blockhouses, timber military structures loopholed and pierced for gunfire. Blockhouses were also a necessity given the frequent and often devastating Native American attacks. There is evidence, in the form of foundations, that Fort James itself featured several row-houses as early as the 1630s.

There were four varieties of seventeenth-century Virginia house plans, representing a not precisely chronological evolution. The simple one-room houses covered about 20 square feet, had brick floors and small windows. The houses were topped by lofts, accessible by ladders. The two-room house was much the same as its New England hall and parlor counterpart, with one significant difference. The New England two-room house was built around a massive central chimney. In the South, two-room houses had chimneys at both ends. The hot climate of the South had something to do with the development of the central-hall plan. A stair to the garret separated hall and parlor, at first a narrow passage, later a larger living space. Such an arrangement took advantage of the cooling effect of cross-ventilation. The first truly unique southern house plan, the cross plan, anticipates some of the features of what would become southern Georgian, especially in its multiple porches. These houses exhibit a wide hall-parlor stretch crossed by a narrower passage containing a projecting vestibule in front and a staircase in back.

Houses of all these varieties might be built of wood or of brick. Wood of many kinds was abundant and popular, including pine, cedar, oak, hickory, and chestnut. Among the original settlers were many bricklayers who capitalized on the region's abundant clay and the lime that could be obtained from local oyster beds. Because of these favorable conditions, brick structures spread more rapidly in the South than in New England. In fact, a rather inscrutable order of 1637 required every owner of 100 or more acres to build a house of brick, perhaps to reduce the risk of fire.

ABOVE: Individuals in Old Salem were permitted to build and live in their own homes, but the building style was determined by the church, which owned the land. *Single Brothers House, Old Salem, North Carolina*

LEFT: The Moravians believed that spiritual growth was demonstrated through the creation of pottery, candles, and other products. *Single Brothers House, Old Salem, North Carolina*

LEFT: The kitchen at Single Brothers House, where unmarried males lived and worshipped together while learning a trade. *Single Brothers House, Old Salem, North Carolina*

RIGHT: Old Salem was established in 1766 under the direction of the Moravian church, a Christian sect from Germany. The church practiced a form of communal living, where members of common sex and marital status lived and worshipped together. *Single Brothers House, Old Salem, North Carolina*

THE SETTLEMENT
OF THE CAROLINAS

The Chesapeake society, that of Virginia and Maryland, began rapidly spreading to the West and South in the early part of the eighteenth century. Fueled by massive migration from Europe, especially of the Scotch-Irish, this trend involved the settling of the back-country inland territories of the South, into the fertile regions of the Carolinas. In addition to a broader spectrum of Europeans than had previously settled the South, the Carolinas also appealed to discontent settlers within the colonies, from Virginia, New England, and the Barbados. In legend, the remote interior of North Carolina was a haven for vagabonds and debtors. In truth, the Carolinas quickly became the fastest growing of the American colonies and far more culturally diverse than Virginia and Maryland.

In the decades prior to the Revolution, population growth in the Carolinas was astonishing. Between 1730 and 1770, the population of North Carolina alone grew from around 30,000 to nearly 200,000. Settlers were generally lower-middle

LEFT: The gardens at Tryon Palace. Governor Tryon's palace, the state capitol, was almost entirely destroyed by fire, marvelous gardens and all, in 1798, and not rebuilt until the 1950s. *Tryon Palace, New Bern, North Carolina*

ABOVE: The finest house in North Carolina was, without much argument from anyone, Governor Tryon's palace at New Bern. Tryon hired esteemed English architect John Hawks to build his palace in 1767. The façade was apparently based on Lord Harcourt's Palladian estate in England. *Tryon Palace, New Bern, North Carolina*

class, perhaps denied opportunities elsewhere. The great fertility and available land in the region allowed many to become successful tobacco farmers. The migration to North Carolina in particular reflected a growing interest in the health and agricultural benefits of non-maritime environments. Although people of many nationalities were drawn to the region, it did not acquire the international character of the northern colonies. Evidence suggests the prevalence of cultural cliques. Scottish Lowlanders and Highlanders kept to their own. The many German settlers in the area were advised not to marry into English and Irish families, to protect their own forms of Protestantism. North Carolina was, at first, a colony without a distinct colonial flavor.

South Carolina, on the other hand, flowered in the eighteenth century into an agrarian high society, centered around Charleston, one of the finest colonial cities of the South. In the seventeenth century, the territory that would become South Carolina was a little-used buffer zone between the English colonies and the hated Spanish settlements in Florida. The foundation of Georgia of 1732 relieved the South Carolina low country of that responsibility, and interest from the north

ABOVE: **Some of the finest examples of North Carolina Georgian architecture, such as the Barker House, can be found in Edenton. Edenton also boasts the Chowan County Courthouse, a fine public building modeled after the old Isle of Wight Courthouse in Smithfield, Virginia.** *Barker House, Edenton, North Carolina*

RIGHT: **British General Cornwallis established his headquarters at what was then the Burgwin house for eighteen days after the Battle of Guilford Courthouse during the Revolutionary War.** *Burgwin-Wright House, Wilmington, North Carolina*

quickly resulted. The South Carolina of the eighteenth century found its major industry in the cultivation of rice and the slave trade associated with it. An enormously profitable crop, rice gave birth to an elite class of planters, not gentlemen by birth, as many Virginian planters were, but instead a kind of upwardly-mobile early American bourgeoisie, an aspirant gentility.

Charleston quickly became the center of a money and pleasure rich society, offering much in the way of amusement and diversion, but little in the way of serious academic pursuits or art. With parties and balls, private clubs, cockfighting, and gambling, Charleston, to some, was perceived as a hedonistic den of sin. It was an area in which lavish displays of wealth were common, wealth that, more than in any other colony, was built on the back of the slave trade. Charleston stands as a reminder of the dichotomies that define the South in general.

GEORGIAN HOUSES OF THE SOUTH

By the end of the seventeenth century, Virginia had become the wealthiest colony in America, in part the result of both slave labor and slave economy. The splendid Georgian homes of the South were more than just houses; they were neighborhoods, virtual communities in and of themselves. In many cases, more than one hundred people lived and worked at a single plantation estate. Such estates often had their own carpenter shops, dairy houses, smokehouses, and even schools. Needless to say, the grounds abounded with elaborate gardens and orchards, fine walls and gates, and smaller homes for farmers, gardeners, and domestic workers.

Some architectural experts suggest that the major Georgian mansions of Virginia, generally regarded as the greatest of all colonial houses, were designed by three men—Richard Taliaferro, John Ariss, and Thomas Jefferson. All three drew from a common pool of influences, notably the example of Andrea Palladio, the Italian architect whose designs were enormously influential in England during the Renaissance revival. The bold symmetricality and regularity of Palladianism was

played out on a grand scale in the wealthy manors of Virginia. Wide doorways were flanked with classical order columns and topped with transom windows. Especially popular was the Palladian window, also known as the Venetian window, a long rectangular window with a small centered arch on top. Palladian windows were quite often placed in the center of the exterior façade, thus one of the primary signifiers of the southern Georgian style.

In 1699, the capital of Virginia moved from Jamestown to Williamsburg after several fires had destroyed prominent state buildings. Freed from the difficult past of Jamestown, the new capital

BELOW: **The venerable port city of Wilmington, North Carolina, offers as its oldest extant residence the Burgwin-Wright House, constructed in 1770 for John Burgwin, treasurer under the Carolina royal governor. The building was constructed on the site of the original town jail, using its stone foundation as a base.** *Burgwin-Wright House, Wilmington, North Carolina*

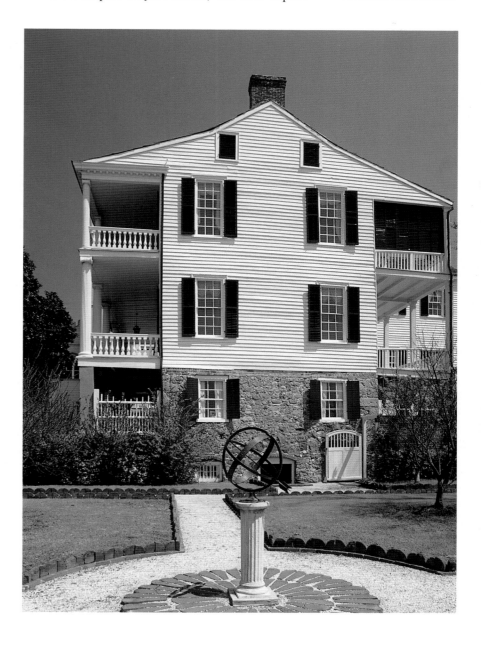

RIGHT: Charleston's Drayton Hall, built between 1738 and 1742, is considered by many to be an innovative specimen of early Georgian architecture, pre-dating even the plantation houses of Virginia in its use of porticoes and other Palladian features which would not appear again in the colonies until the 1750s. *Drayton Hall, Charleston, South Carolina*

RIGHT: The current Kershaw-Cornwallis house is a beautifully executed reconstruction of the original structure, which was destroyed in 1865 during the Union occupation of Camden. *Kershaw-Cornwallis House, Camden, South Carolina*

RIGHT: The Cupola House in Edenton is architecturally significant in that it is the only surviving house in the South featuring a second-story overhang. Scholars consider the Cupola House to be a prime example of a building squarely in between the colonial and Georgian styles. *Cupola House, Edenton, North Carolina*

ABOVE: **Few colonial structures rival the Governor's Palace in terms of detail and complexity. The magnificent estate was home to a remarkable succession of figures in American history, including Patrick Henry and Thomas Jefferson.** *The Governor's Palace, Williamsburg, Virginia*

quickly rose to display the new affluence and refinement of southern culture, and stands today as a museum of fine early Georgian architecture. Like Philadelphia, though much smaller, Williamsburg was a planned city, designed by Theordorick Bland to fit into a gridiron modeled after Renaissance European cities. The central axis of the plan was the Duke of Gloucester Street, a very wide street that connected two of the most important architectural landmarks of the city: the Capitol on the east end, and the College of William and Mary on the west.

The most impressive house in Williamsburg, and at the time of its completion, perhaps the most impressive in all of America, is the Governor's Palace, constructed between 1706 and 1720 by Henry Cary. With its astonishing English gardens, stone-carved lion and unicorn gateway, hedge maze, bowling green, lagoon,

and massive ballroom with crystal chandeliers, the Governor's Palace clearly demonstrates that royalist pretension was stronger in the South than in any other region of colonial America, even though it claims both Patrick Henry and Thomas Jefferson as residents. The Governor's Palace, and Williamsburg in general, provided the model upon which many of the great Virginian plantation estates would be based: Mount Airy in Richmond, George Washington's home at Mount Vernon, and Thomas Jefferson's Monticello, among many others.

Not all of the fine southern mansions are to be found in Virginia. Similarly grand specimens also abound in Annapolis, Maryland, and in the Charleston area of South Carolina. Unlike earlier colonial days, regional styles were not terribly distinct. Architectural standards among the wealthy, those most likely to own Georgian

LEFT: A product of the prosperity of the southern tobacco trade, the Governor's Palace at Williamsburg, Virginia, stands as a classic example of Christopher Wren-influenced Georgian architecture. *The Governor's Palace, Williamsburg, Virginia*

homes, were fairly consistent. However separated by cultural differences, cities such as Boston and Annapolis were united in their reliance upon standard texts on classical architecture and Palladianism. In Maryland, the most sophisticated houses owe their existence to William Buckland, an English-born architect who designed many of the finest houses of Annapolis. In addition to being an inspired architect, Buckland was apparently also a skilled carver and joiner, and the houses he is credited with building (or is surmised to have built) reveal unusually fine woodwork detail.

The Civil War, countless hurricanes, and economic problems have denied present day tourists the chance to enjoy many of the great houses of South Carolina, although Charleston remains a fine example of a colonial city. It is in Charleston that the universal standards of the Georgian meet

and breed with what has come to be known as southern style—a style characterized by warm brick and stucco exteriors, red-tiled roofs, and wrought-iron balconies. Of special historical interest is the Miles Brewton House, which, after its owners died at sea, served as British headquarters during the Revolutionary War.

The architectural history of the South vividly demonstrates that political and artistic trends do not always run parallel. While revolutionary ideology and intentions spread widely throughout the colonies, the spirit of southern architecture grew ever more English and aristocratic in character. Even Thomas Jefferson, the most eloquent spokesmen of the revolutionary American ideals, looked to the great traditions of European architecture for his inspiration. Thus did the American style grow from a studious and selective adaptation of many European heritages.

FOLLOWING PAGE: Inside and outside, Mount Vernon abounds with fine classical detail. Like Jefferson at Monticello, Washington regarded a home as a life's work in progress. After his final term as president, Washington said, "I had rather be at Mount Vernon with a friend or two about me, than to be attended at the seat of government by the officers of state and the representatives of every power in Europe." *Mount Vernon, Fairfax County, Virginia*

RIGHT: The west parlor at Mount Vernon remains one of the finest surviving examples of colonial Virginia interiors. The room was the center of the Washingtons' social life, and the walls are adorned with family portraits. *Mount Vernon, Fairfax County, Virginia*

RIGHT: The large dining room at Mount Vernon— the home of George Washington from 1754 until his death in 1799— is said to have been his favorite. The room is two stories high, and the ceiling is decorated with agricultural motifs. *Mount Vernon, Fairfax County, Virginia*

LEFT: The downstairs bedroom at Mount Vernon, where the Washingtons' many overnight guests were likely to have stayed. *Mount Vernon, Fairfax County, Virginia*

LEFT: Much of the woodwork in the Mount Vernon study—as well as the rest of the mansion—was of pine, painted to simulate a finer wood. *Mount Vernon, Fairfax County, Virginia*

ABOVE: In the late years of the eighteenth century, Washington's Mount Vernon home grew in almost every possible direction, including upward. In 1759, the roof was raised from one-and-a-half to two-and-a-half stories. *Mount Vernon, Fairfax County, Virginia*

RIGHT: One of the final additions to Washington's Mount Vernon was also, literally, its crowning touch. The famous Cupola was added in 1778, two years after the north and south additions had been completed. *Mount Vernon, Fairfax County, Virginia*

AFTERWORD

COLONIAL REVIVALS

The words colonial revival might seem to imply that, starting in the late nineteenth century, Americans resumed building two-room timber houses and log cabins or living in dugouts on the Chesapeake. Colonial revival, however, refers not to the colonial style of architecture, but to the revival of the dominant style of architecture in the colonial, pre-revolution years—in other words, the Georgian. The colonial revival coincides with the reawakening of interest in American antecedents, with an increased sense of national spirit and patriotism. It has proved to be an enduringly popular style. If Georgian architecture was originally the cultural property of the English and their interpretation of classicism, the proliferation of colonial-style houses in the United States during the nineteenth and twentieth centuries was and continues to be uniquely American.

Since its beginnings in the 1870s, the colonial revival, however misnamed, has become one of the most popular architectural styles in American history. The reasons for this phenomenon are many and varied. Most explanations begin by identifying colonial revival as a reaction to the styles and fashions of architecture, as well as to social and cultural trends that had taken shape in nineteenth-century America. Perhaps the new interest in and passion for all things colonial represented a widespread cultural reaction to the industrial revolution, to the accelerated beginnings of the modern world. The colonial revival was, in part, a gasping for breath, a symbolic return to simpler styles and simpler needs.

The colonial revival was also a specific reaction to Victorian architectural excess, especially to the decorative indulgence known as the Queen Anne house. American architects were rediscovering classicism under the pervasive influence of the Ecole des Beaux Arts in France. This led to a reconsideration and renewal of American architectural traditions. Reawakened interest in American classicism brought architects and scholars to a most disturbing discovery. The classic early specimens of American architecture had not been treated well in the intervening years. Among the other motives and outcomes of the colonial revival were a new respect for American traditions and a new emphasis on preservation.

The architects of the colonial revival faced major challenges when it came to adapting colonial characteristics to modern needs. In many cases, the homage to colonialism was superficial, a façade stuck on an otherwise thoroughly modern house. Those Americans who wanted colonial homes did not necessarily want colonial conditions. They were, after all, usually wealthy individuals who required much space and flexibility in their homes. Thus, the vast majority of early colonial revival houses were hardly accurate replicas of the originals. They were, for one thing, generally much bigger. They may have borrowed the symmetrical shapes of Georgian architecture, but the towers, bays, and verandahs of the Queen Anne remained popular in early colonial revivals.

The early colonial revival craze was primarily the territory of the wealthy, those who could afford to decide what kind of house they lived in, and what kind of statement it made. Georgian features such as columns, gable roofs, and modillion cornices returned to popularity. Solid-panel shutters flanked windows. Houses sat low to the ground. Interiors, too, reflected a return to simpler values and aesthetics. Accompanying a general trend away from ornamental clutter was the return of the central hall. As the colonial revival progressed, it generally became more authentically colonial—bold and simple in design and furnishing.

The colonial revival peaked in popularity in the early twentieth century and corresponds to the growth of the American middle class, when colonial style became less a signifier of the elite and more the architectural staple of rapidly expanding suburban America. The colonial revival homes that filled the post-World War I suburbs, block after block of often mass-produced homes, were, in some sense, a more genuine adaptation of colonial styles and values than the first revivals built for and by wealthy Americans. The features of the American colonial house are so common, so accepted that now they have ceased to be colonial and ceased to be revivals. They are simply American.

ABOVE: George Washington's home at Mount Vernon underwent continual development and transformation between 1757 and Washington's death on December 14, 1799. Although it began as a modest farmhouse created by an unknown designer, Mount Vernon as it stands today is perhaps the United States' finest example of the grand Palladian villa. *Mount Vernon, Fairfax County, Virginia*

INDEX

Page numbers in **bold-face** type indicate photo captions.